Fashions of a
Decade
The 1960s

Fashions of a Decade
The 1960s

Yvonne Connikie

CHELSEA HOUSE
PUBLISHERS
An imprint of Infobase Publishing

Chelsea House
An imprint of Infobase Publishing
132 West 31st Street
New York NY 10001

For Library of Congress Cataloging-in-Publication Data
please contact the publisher.
ISBN 0-8160-6722-8

Chelsea House books are available at special discounts when purchased in bulk quantities for businesses, associations, institutions, or sales promotions. Please call our Special Sales Department in New York at (212) 967-8800 or (800) 322-8755.

You can find Chelsea House on the World Wide Web at
http://www.chelseahouse.com

Author: Yvonne Connikie
Research for new edition: Kathy Elgin
Editor: Karen Taschek
Text design by Simon Borrough
Cover design by Dorothy M.Preston
Illustrations by Robert Price
Picture Research by Shelley Noronha

This new edition produced for Chelsea House by Bailey Publishing Associates Ltd.

Printed in China through Morris Press, Ltd.

CP SB 10 9 8 7 6 5 4 3 2 1

This book is printed on acid-free paper.

Contents

	Introduction	6
1	Cocktails and Beehives	28
2	The Beatnik Generation	32
3	The Beatles: Pop Goes Fashion	36
4	Motown, Mods and Minis	40
5	The Space Age	44
6	The Ethnic Look	48
7	Psychedelic Explosion	52
8	Flower Power Goes High Fashion	56
	Chronology	60
	Glossary	62
	Further Reading	63
	Acknowledgments	63
	Index	64

The 60s

The 1960s were a great time to be young. Youth culture and youth fashions, which had begun to take shape in the fifties, blossomed as never before. Young people in the West were benefiting from the postwar industrial boom and had begun to refashion themselves accordingly. The existing fashion business wasn't always able or willing to deal with this shift in demand, so the youth market would largely belong to a new generation of designers. Fashion split the age groups.

Extra cash in young people's pockets meant extra freedom—freedom for the imagination, freedom for creative and provocative ideas. The world was becoming a smaller place as people began to take the idea of the global village for granted. The new freedom of youth made itself felt on both sides of the Atlantic, and it also began to make ripples farther afield—in Japan, Africa, and Eastern Europe.

Pop Stars

Pop music also went through enormous changes—people even began to take it seriously as an art form. The charts were virtually taken over by young, even teenage artists, who were making the music young listeners most wanted to hear. Biggest of all were the Beatles, four young men from Liverpool, England, who had begun by playing to packed nightclubs in England and Germany before storming the world stage in 1963. The Beatles' clothes and hairstyles became the most familiar symbols of the new youth culture.

Although the Beatles were the most popular group, they were strongly challenged as spokesmen for youth by two other figures: singer-songwriter Bob Dylan and Mick Jagger of the Rolling Stones. Both Dylan and the Stones opted for a rebellious look, wearing outfits that recalled the outlaws of western or gangster movies—and in fact, both Dylan and Jagger have acted in such films. They gave form to Yves Saint Laurent's remark that "clothes were a form of protest," and both acquired a host of imitators.

In the mid-sixties, Motown, a record company under African American ownership, began to take a dominant share of the singles charts. Motown launched the careers of megastars like Diana Ross, Smokey Robinson, Michael Jackson, and Stevie Wonder. Instead of taking a rebellious stance, Motown promoted a smart, stylish, and upwardly mobile image, insisting on extensive grooming and styling for its artists before public appearances. The alliance of fashion with pop music has never been closer.

All these artists created their own distinctive styles of dress. Dylan developed from beatnik to hippie to suede-jacketed country rocker. The Beatles moved from chic Pierre Cardin suits to the spaced-out military uniforms of the *Sgt. Pepper* period. The Rolling Stones posed as threatening, deliberately unkempt delinquents. Motown girl groups like the Supremes dressed themselves

Rock Stars

Rock stars in the 1960s gained an importance that went well beyond the audience for their music. Performers like Bob Dylan, Mick Jagger, Janis Joplin, and Jimi Hendrix were seen as speaking on behalf of the younger generation—both by young people themselves and by the media, who sought out their views on any and every issue. Often the stars themselves were annoyed by the pressures they felt were being placed on them—"I'm not the leader of no organization" commented an angry Dylan. Jagger and Hendrix, among others, spent time behind bars on drug charges, and both were considered to have received harsher treatment from the courts because, as figures in the public eye, it was thought to be worth making an example of them.

▲The Supremes, immaculately dressed in furs, arrive at London airport in 1965. On stage or off, they were never anything less than elegant.

◄ Bob Dylan, the James Dean of his generation, in fringed cowboy jacket and jeans,somewhere between hippie and rock star.

up in gloves, satins, and feather boas; male groups like the Temptations and the Four Tops went for color-coordinated suits. Everything these artists were expressing about their music and attitudes could be understood at a glance through their clothes. And the freedom that fashion allowed meant that everyone could dress up. All young people, in fact, could think of themselves as performers and "do their own thing."

Out of the Fifties

But the sixties had begun in a very different mood. The year 1960 seemed not so different from 1959, and the atmosphere of the late fifties lingered on until the explosion of new energy around 1963. To understand this period, we need to look at what had gone before.

Fifties fashion had been dominated by two strands that completely failed to connect—the styles of the great haute couture fashion houses and the sudden emergence of the teenager and teenage fashions. The fifties were in many ways also the heyday of the great Paris fashion houses like Dior, Givenchy, Lanvin, and Balenciaga. They continued to dictate new styles of fashion season by season. Tailoring and finishing were carried out to the very highest standards, as was the case with their fashion rivals in New York, London, and Rome. A more youthful approach was being taken by the young French designer Yves Saint Laurent, who began designing under his own label in 1962. Although Saint Laurent's ideas might have been radical and new, he was seen at first as simply the latest in a long line of Paris masters of cut and style. And in the fifties, high fashion remained largely the preserve of the wealthy, making relatively little impact on the dress of the average office worker.

▲The movie version of *West Side Story*, hitting the screen in 1961, was a timely reminder that teenage street violence and racial tensions were still high on the agenda.

◄ Bare feet, "Sloppy Joe" sweater, tight pants, and outrageous behavior—in 1960, it could only spell beatnik.

▲ The Rolling Stones, looking cool but rebellious at the Mod Ball in 1964.

Poles apart from all this were the youth cults that sprang up, often considered as dangerous breeding grounds for juvenile delinquency. American teenage style and its dangers were reflected in the hit movie *West Side Story*. Standing apart from this were the beatniks, who jumped to prominence in the late fifties, particularly in California and New York. The beat culture was primarily a movement of writers, with Jack Kerouac, Allen Ginsberg, and Lawrence Ferlinghetti some of its leading lights. Certain styles of dress (and a leaning toward hard-bop jazz) were a fixed part of the beatnik attitude: handmade sandals, black turtleneck sweaters, black berets, and tight black pants. The beatniks' "outsider" or bohemian attitudes, mixing up popular culture with "high art," were a foretaste of what the sixties would offer. The beatniks themselves spilled over into the new decade—in fact, the beatnik philosophy has never really gone away.

The couture look for the start of the decade can be seen in Dior's woven straw hat, black stiletto heels, black beads, and gauntlet gloves. The formality of the model's pose matches the restrained elegance of the setting.

►Was this the most exclusive suit of all? As Buzz Aldrin takes his historic moonwalk on July 20 1969, Neil Armstrong and the lunar module can be seen reflected in his face mask.

►And this was how they did it in the movies. The Stanley Kubrick and Arthur C. Clarke sci-fi vision *2001: A Space Odyssey* pre-dated Aldrin's real-life adventure by a year.

Space Race

In the early sixties, the Soviet Union seemed to be well ahead of the United States in the race to space. In 1961, Soviet cosmonaut Yuri Gagarin completed one orbit of the earth in the spacecraft Vostok 1. President Kennedy declared publicly that the United States would catch up, and in 1962, John Glenn became the first US astronaut to orbit the earth, as part of the Mercury space program. The United States followed up the Mercury flights with the two-man Gemini spacecraft and finally the three-man Apollo project. Apollo 8's flight during Christmas 1968 placed men for the first time in orbit around the moon—by far the most spectacular spaceflight to date. This feat was surpassed in July 1969, when Apollo 11 landed two of its crew on the surface of the moon, fulfilling Kennedy's pledge of a manned moon landing before the end of the decade. By contrast, the Soviet space program seemed to have lost its way after its early successes, which had included the first "space walk," by Aleksei Leonov in 1965.

Mod Cult

The new decade had begun to show its true face by 1963. This was the year of worldwide Beatlemania, and it was also the year that the mod cult—short for "moderns"—erupted in Britain. Mods personified the early years of the Swinging Sixties—youth, mobility (mods lived by their motor scooters), fashion (they spared no expense on their clothes), and an intense interest in soul and R & B, particularly Booker T. and Wilson Pickett. But by 1964 a series of pitched battles at British seaside resorts between groups of mods and rival rockers—"greaser" motorcycle gangs—had given mods a bad name. By the mid-sixties, they had begun to fade out.

▲It was a weekend tradition that large groups of mods, dressed in sharp suits, narrow ties, and "parka" anoraks, and riding shiny chrome-trimmed scooters, would invade the popular British seaside resort of Brighton.

▼The typical American family at home in front of the TV. Although color broadcasts began in 1954, there were far fewer channels than we have today.

Science and Technology

The "affluent society" of the West meant that more and more technological gadgets became commonplace during the sixties: color television, hi-fi record players, better cars, and more sophisticated washing machines. Cheaper jet air travel led to an enormous boom in tourism. Giant strides were being made in computer technology, bringing the first desktop computers in sight, and also in medicine, with the first heart transplant operations being performed. Scientific progress seemed to be unstoppable: anything seemed possible in the years ahead.

Quant Cult

What didn't fade away was the mod enthusiasm for young, stylish fashions. The boy on the motor scooter was replaced by the girl in her miniskirt—a fashion breakthrough that was to maintain its importance until the end of the decade. The term "youth-quake" was widely heard. One of the first designers to take advantage of this rapidly changing atmosphere was Mary Quant.

▼Twiggy, undeniably the face of the sixties.

▲ PVC (polyvinyl chloride), in its soft form, was a favorite of the mid-sixties fashion industry. Raincoats in bright primary colors or bold checks, paired with sou'wester hats, were a jaunty response to the weather.

▲Diana Rigg as hard-hitting agent Emma Peel in the cult series *The Avengers*. Her outrageous outfits—especially the high, "kinky" boots—quickly became mainstreet fashion spin-offs.

▲Young fashions from Rive Gauche in 1967.

Changing Times for Women?

The postwar era of the late forties and fifties had seen most women in the West still tied—or returning after war work—to the roles of wife and mother, although the new availability of domestic gadgets did make these roles less physically demanding than before. But the turbulent social atmosphere of the sixties led to a belief that anything was possible—even a complete revolution in the relationships between men and women. Easily available and reliable contraception offered women far greater control over their personal relationships. By the end of the decade, however, women had made only modest progress in terms of representation in politics, business, or the professions. Indeed, many of the fashions and values of the sixties tended to push young women into a vulnerable or passive "dumb blonde" role. A pretty girl in a miniskirt wasn't expected to say anything intelligent.

Quant had been designing and manufacturing her own clothes since the late fifties, but the young, fun fashions she designed began to take off in the atmosphere of the early sixties. Her high point was undoubtedly the launch of the miniskirt—a fashionable skirt that rose eight or nine inches above the knee and stayed there, at least until the arrival of maxi and midi lengths in 1969–70. Like Saint Laurent, Quant moved away from the traditional role of the fashion designer, producing her own collection of tights with open-mesh designs and original lace effects and starting her own range of cosmetics. Tights (in place of

►Yves Saint Laurent's new Rive Gauche boutique on the Champs-Elysées.

◄ "It is given to a fortunate few to be born at the right time, in the right place, with the right talents. In recent fashion there are three: Chanel, Dior, and Mary Quant [pictured]." Ernestine Carter, in London's *Sunday Times.*

▲Many of the new, young British designers were fresh out of college and started out working in surprisingly small quarters before their businesses took off. Here Mary Quant pins a new design on her model.

stockings) were essential with the miniskirt and, along with the softer, wireless bra, pointed the way for women's underwear.

Mary Quant was also closely involved with the sixties revolution in shopping habits. From the mid-decade on, Europe and North America began to fill up with boutiques—small clothing shops aimed at the teenage customer and depending on a rapid turnover of stock. Shopping for clothes became fun. Mary Quant's Bazaar chain in the United Kingdom, which opened in the late fifties, was described by Quant herself as "a kind of permanently running cocktail party." Yves Saint Laurent was on the same wavelength: his boutique chain Rive Gauche, which opened in 1966, quickly expanded to 160 branches worldwide. Other designers soon followed suit.

Beach Boys (and Girls Too)

The Swinging Sixties/space-age mood caught on fast in the United States. Betsey Johnson attracted attention with her gangster-stripe pantsuits and clear-vinyl dress with paste-on-yourself stars, while Rudi Gernreich covered all the bases first by producing the world's first topless swimsuit and then by pairing a strappy bathing suit with thigh-high boots and a space-visor. Few actually went topless, but swimwear and the bikini in particular became briefer than ever. Established

Violent Societies

Despite all the talk of peace and love, the world of the sixties seemed to be as violent as ever. Full-scale wars raged in Southeast Asia, in the Middle East, and on the Indian subcontinent. Soviet tanks entered Czechoslovakia to crush Prime Minister Dubcek's liberalizing government. British troops were on the streets of Northern Ireland from August 1969. Riots flared up in Los Angeles, Chicago, Paris, and Berlin. Other people pointed to increasing crime and lawlessness: Richard Nixon found the law-and-order ticket useful in gaining entry to the White House. Assassinations also made the headlines. The most prominent public figures to be gunned down were John F. Kennedy, Robert Kennedy, and Dr. Martin Luther King, Jr. Street crime began to be discussed as a serious problem in some of the world's major cities. The future might have arrived, but it didn't seem to be a peaceful one.

designers Geoffrey Beene and Anne Fogarty also used the miniskirt to their advantage, Beene teaming up short skirts with long jackets and Fogarty introducing her "mini-culottes."

Mods were never much in evidence in the United States: American youth had been enjoying the cult of the automobile since the fifties. The early sixties music of the Beach Boys and others tended to put cars first and girls second, as suggested by the Beach Boys' song "Little Deuce Coupe." Surf music favored an easy, casual dressing style suitable for California sunshine, and short-sleeved, open-neck striped shirts were the favorite attire of the Beach Boys themselves, along with carefully waved hair. The flavor of this period is perfectly captured by the costumes and sound track of the 1973 film *American Graffiti*, which reflects a teenager's need to leave behind his comfortable small-town life for the bigger world outside.

▲*American Graffiti*, directed by George Lucas (1973), brilliantly re-created the atmosphere of 1960s small-town America.

▶The Beach Boys' clean-cut, casual image perfectly matched their bright, accessible close-harmony songs, focusing on sun, sand, and surfing.

◀ Culottes for spring 1967, from the Relang collection. Although they were much favored by designers at this time, culottes never rivaled the popularity of the miniskirt.

Cold War?

The Cold War between the US and USSR. nearly became "hot" in 1962, when presidents Kennedy and Khrushchev clashed over the placement of Soviet nuclear missiles in Cuba, just ninety miles off the Florida coastline. With the two countries sliding towards the brink of war, Khrushchev backed down and agreed to remove the missiles. The Cuban Crisis also marked the end of Khrushchev's political career. A new, more cautious regime in Moscow, headed by Prime Minister Alexsei Kosygin and Party Chairman Leonid Brezhnev, seemed content to watch and wait as the US entangled itself ever more deeply in the Vietnam War. Both superpowers, however, watched the unfolding of China's Cultural Revolution with alarm: a new and unpredictable superpower suited neither of them. And while neither the US nor USSR wanted war with each other, both continued throughout the decade to stockpile ever more powerful nuclear weapons.

Peace and War

For many small-town American youths, however, the bigger world outside found them—in the shape of the draft and a year of duty in Vietnam. The average age of the American soldiers killed in Vietnam was just nineteen, a statistic that helps explain the increasingly political nature of American youth culture from the mid-sixties on. Musicians like folk singers Joan Baez and Pete Seeger spoke out publicly against the war, and warned of even worse catastrophe should anything like the Cuban missile crisis—when the United States and the Soviet Union were in direct confrontation—be repeated in Southeast Asia. While students

Vietnam

In the fifties, fighting in Vietnam—then known as "French Indo-China"—had involved French troops and the Vietcong nationalist forces. A cease-fire had divided the country in two. In the early sixties, the United States was drawn into renewed fighting on the side of the non-Communist south, with President Kennedy making the initial decision to send in troops. By the mid-sixties the United States found itself heavily committed to a costly war that was unpopular both at home and abroad. Indeed, Kennedy's successor, Lyndon Johnson, lost so much support because of his commitment to the war that he elected not to run for office a second time in 1968. The Vietnam War was the cause of sharp divisions and unrest in American society, and it provided a strong political focus to many young people. The war was a particularly bitter experience for many African-Americans, with leaders like Eldridge Cleaver and Huey Newton pointing to the contradiction of African-Americans being sent to defend democracy in Southeast Asia while their battle for civil rights was not yet won at home.

▲ The Reverend Martin Luther King Jr., assassinated in 1968, led the civil rights movement throughout the sixties. At huge outdoor gatherings, he held thousands of African-Americans spellbound by his impassioned rhetoric.

◄ Muhammad Ali, world heavyweight boxing champion and perhaps the sixties' most famous Black Muslim. Ali refused the Vietnam draft and was later stripped of his world title.

▲ Joan Baez was one of the foremost protest singers, appearing at student meetings all over the country as well as making records

demonstrated against the war and the draft, other Americans were horrified by the live images of fighting brought into their homes for the first time by television. By the end of the decade, US forces were beginning to pull out of Vietnam.

Hippie Power

The hippie ideals of peace and love have often been ridiculed in the years since the sixties, but it is worth remembering that the movement grew up against a backdrop of compulsory military service, at least in the United States, where the hippie movement had its roots. Hippiedom was worldwide, and all you had to do to join was to let your hair grow. Although members of what was at bottom a

▲Demonstrations against the Vietnam War spread throughout Europe. Many, like this one held in London in 1968, began peacefully but ended in violence.

political and moral movement rejecting Western materialism and its money hungry "rat race," hippies set the tone for much of the fashion of the late sixties. They set the seal on the "anything goes" attitude, which had been building in force for some time, happily mixing up ethnic and psychedelic influences. In fact, the hippies had such a widespread impact that by the early seventies, long hair and ethnic wear had become just another way of dressing up, with little or no political significance attached.

Hippie dress fitted in with the new "peacock" attitude to male dress, considered suitable for a society moving toward greater equality between the sexes. Men either dressed up as a form of self-expression or to attract women,

◀ In 1968, rioting students tore Paris apart. The baton-swinging security police, seen here clearing the Boulevard Saint Michel, showed little sympathy with their demands.

▼ Sly and the Family Stone's afro hairstyles were as startling as the unprecedented funkiness of their music, which pointed the way forward to the dance music of the seventies and eighties.

just as women had always dressed up to attract men. The declining infant mortality rate meant that for the first time in history, there were more men than women to go around. Men needed to compete with one another to gain attention, while women were taking advantage of the chance to dress more simply, in practical pantsuits—and especially jeans. "You can't tell the boys from the girls these days" was a frequent complaint. "Unisex" dressing was the style: young hippie men and women wore their hair long, with headbands, and dressed in worn-out jeans. Anything, in fact, that was not "neat."

A Shrinking World

Another by-product of hippie culture was the general acceptance of varied styles of "ethnic" dress, although the prime movers in this area were black musicians and the Black Power organizations. African-American pop

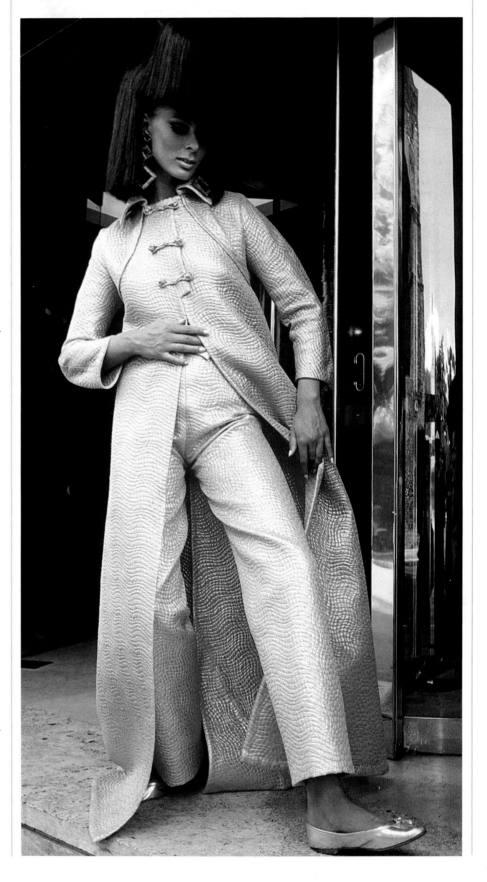

► A vaguely oriental ethnic look combines with the space-age influence in this 1967 Vancetti pantsuit. Note the textured, quilted-look fabric and the wildly experimental hairstyling.

stars in particular began to drop the carefully groomed Caucasian style and allow themselves to project a much stronger black image: Sly and the Family Stone and Isaac Hayes are good examples. Established artists like Martha and the Vandellas altered their image, while hard-core soul artists like James Brown began to attract a mainstream following. As the black ethnic look became more popular, "afro" hairstyles spread as far afield as Japan.

The ethnic mood was also fueled by cheaper and more ambitious travel, with exotic places like Bali and Nepal suddenly becoming realistic destinations. The focus of fashion was beginning to extend beyond Europe and North America. The world might be getting smaller, but the fashion map was becoming more diverse all the time.

A False Impression

As the decade ended, American, French, and Italian designers—especially Pucci, Vancetti, and Saint Laurent—were at the forefront of those seeking to transform street fashions into designer collections. Bonnie Cashin's work had used ethnic garments like the poncho as early as the late fifties, followed by Betsey Johnson, with her cowhide minidresses. The Italian designer Fiorucci began establishing his own personal niche halfway between boutique fashion and the designer label.

Nevertheless, by the end of the sixties, it was clear that fashion had not changed as completely as many had believed. Some landmarks had gone, including Balenciaga, the last of the great "pure" couturiers, who retired in 1968. But many of the old-guard fashion elite were still around, and big names like Chanel continued on their established course almost as if the Swinging Sixties had never happened. The French had hardly taken a back-seat during the decade, with Courrèges and Cardin cashing in on both the space-age and Op Art fever and keeping only half a step behind the London designers in promoting the miniskirt. Paris might have been eclipsed in the sixties, but the city was set to make a big comeback in the seventies and eighties.

The Apollo 11 moon landing in 1969 gave a timely end-of-decade boost to all things space age, but the end of the sixties saw the first signs of a new conservatism, both in fashion and in society. Richard Nixon was elected president in 1968, promising to speak on behalf of the "silent majority." France turned away from radical politics after the student uprisings of 1968, while Britain elected a new Conservative government in 1970. And just as the 1960s had seen fashion reach forward into the future, rushing to embrace new or exotic ideas, the seventies were to be gripped by a very different mood: a nostalgic yearning for the past.

Woodstock

It began as the 1969 Woodstock Free Festival of Art and Music, and it ended as the biggest event of its kind the world had ever seen, with crowds estimated at half a million. A movie and two double albums attempted to package the atmosphere of an event in which Jimi Hendrix, Sly and the Family Stone, The Who, Santana, Janis Joplin, and many others performed. The event became bigger than the music and turned into a symbol of everything connected with hippies, flower children, and the "love generation." An attempt to repeat the success of Woodstock on the West Coast at Altamont later in 1969 ended in disaster when a spectator tried to fire a shot at Mick Jagger while the Rolling Stones were performing on stage. The man was killed by members of a Hell's Angels motorcycle gang, which the Stones had hired as a security force.

▶August 1969. The Woodstock festival, in upstate New York, was the place to be that summer: camping out under the stars at the biggest rock concert ever conceived. What the festival planners hadn't anticipated was 500,000 people.

Cocktails and Beehives

We'll Always Have Paris

John F. Kennedy became president in January 1960, and his fashionable and glamorous wife, Jackie, became the new first lady. Much younger than their predecessors, the Kennedys were seen by many as signs of a new hope and optimism for the new decade.

Jackie Kennedy became a prominent style-setter for the latest French fashions. Yves Saint Laurent opened his own fashion house in 1962 and quickly enhanced his reputation as the most innovative and brilliant of the younger designers. Coco Chanel, fifty years into her career, maintained her reputation for shunning all extremes, although she did promote a shorter-length lacy cocktail dress and went along with the trend for leaner, narrower cuts.

Still going strong from the fifties was the "bouffant" look, with skirts supported by underlayers of stiff petticoats. This style was developed into the "*suspense-jupe*," with the ballooning fullness of the skirt constricted at the knee.

▲Another Christian Dior cocktail/evening look for 1962. There is a touch of the "*suspense-jupe*" in the cut of the skirt, which is gathered tightly at the waist and tapers to the hem.

◄ First lady Jackie Kennedy, wearing one of her famous pillbox hats and a wool bouclé suit. Her charm and chic sophistication conquered world leaders and charmed diplomats wherever she and the president went.

▲This 1960 cocktail dress, Italian style, looks like the last gasp of fifties fashion. Note also the overall formality, seen in the model, the setting, and the spectators alongside the catwalk.

▲ Girl-next-door Doris Day maintained her own brand of sophistication offscreen.

For some years, it had been fashionable to pull the hair back off the face. Suddenly, hair came alive with back combing (teasing) and the arrival of the "beehive," a fuller shape kept in place with plenty of hair spray. Women enjoyed the new freedom, wearing their hair loose, or piled on top of the head in a bun. Those with short hair achieved the same effect with hair pieces.

Move Over, Darling

Men's styles at this time were strongly influenced by Italian designers. Formality was still the keynote, even for leisure wear. Suits were single breasted, featuring short jackets with narrow lapels, worn over narrow-collar shirts and slim ties. Pants were narrower, especially for the young and fashionable, with the tapering effect finished off with pointed "winkle-picker" shoes. Longer hair for men was beginning to replace the short back and sides but was still firmly slicked back with oil and gel. As facial hair became more acceptable, men of all ages grew lavish mustaches and beards, and many let their sideburns grow fuller and longer.

Many teenage girls, especially in Europe, were still wearing clothes almost identical to their mothers'. The big revolution in teenage fashion still lay in the future. Many copied the look projected by Hollywood star Doris Day, a pretty, feminine image that appealed to women of all ages. Doris Day combined a girl-next-door appearance with a glamorous and stylish movie-star image, and in movies like *The Thrill of It All* and *Move Over, Darling*, she became the biggest box office draw of the period. The music and style of these films is often used to re-create the atmosphere of the early sixties.

Let's Twist Again!

Elsewhere, music still rocked and rolled, and couples jived and danced the latest crazes like the Mashed Potato or the Twist. You needed to know the right steps, which were

▲Custom-made tailoring for men remained a strong tradition, but styling went through rapid change. This 1964 suit by Hector Powe would look good on sixties fictional heroes like James Bond or Napoleon Solo from *The Man from U.N.C.L.E.* Typical details include draped shoulders, wide lapels, button-down collar, and crocodile zip boots.

▲Top girl group the Ronettes pose in all-blue formal outfits and carefully back-combed beehive hairstyles.

all mapped out in magazines, ready to be copied on Saturday night. And if couples weren't twisting to Chubby Checker, they might well be smooching to ballads by Gene Pitney, Helen Shapiro, or even former rocker Elvis Presley, who returned from army service with a new, clean-cut image and romantic songs like "It's Now or Never," a reworking of the Italian ballad "O sole mio."

The sixties looked set to continue very much in the vein of the previous decade: new faces, new fashions, but little change in the underlying mood. But no one writing in, say, 1960 could have foreseen the enormous changes and reversals that lay in the years ahead.

▶ A wool day wear suit by Dior, from 1963. Blouse and jacket feature a typically wide, rounded collar line, and the outfit is completed by the still-obligatory hat and gloves.

The Beatnik Generation

Left Bank Paris

Under their calm and conservative surface, the fifties had been a period of enormous change for artists and designers. By the end of the decade, some of this energy was beginning to show itself in the changing moods of jazz, cinema, and fashion.

In the Saint Germain quarter of Paris, the Left Bank movement had emerged as long ago as the forties, led by a group of writers and artists who tried to live their daily lives according to their radical new ideas, challenging established values and conventions. Philosopher Jean-Paul Sartre and feminist Simone de Beauvoir were at the center of a circle that attracted a wider group of "bohemians," including film directors François Truffaut and Roger Vadim and jazz singer Juliette Greco.

Juliette Greco was a Left Bank fashion symbol, whether dressed in slacks and black beret or her black Balmain evening dress. The bohemians of Saint Germain gathered together to see Greco and visiting American jazz stars at notorious nightclubs like Le Tabou and Le Rose Rouge—notorious, that is, to non-bohemians. Another Left Bank style model was Brigitte Bardot, dressed in a tight-fitting black-and-white T-shirt or pouting from behind a tangle of curls.

▲The jacket for Donald Byrd's *Byrd in Hand* album, released in 1959 but selling well into the next decade, shows the trumpeter in typical jazz-man's casual turtleneck.

▶Juliette Greco, jazz heroine of the Paris Left Bank, caught in a self-reflective pose.

▼A typical beatnik house in Liverpool in 1960: perhaps not that different from the average student room.

San Francisco, Heart of the Beats

Far away in California, something similar had been going on, taking its cue from young, experimental writers like Jack Kerouac and Allen Ginsberg. Their style of writing was fast and spontaneous. Kerouac described his books *On the Road* (1957) and *The Subterraneans* (1958) as having been "written on the run," while beat poet Ginsberg believed in live performances to "capture an audience."

Beatniks were "hip," "cool," and "groovy" and considered themselves in rebellion against the "square" world of the establishment. "Hip" could be anything from be-bop jazz to Buddhism to just walking in a particular way, defined as "a catlike walk from the hips." "Hip" also meant turning away from the dress and even the speech of the white middle class toward the music and culture of black America.

Paris and San Francisco remained the twin centers of the beatnik universe, but groups of beatniks or beatnik imitators sprang up in towns across the world. The beat style included black berets, black slacks, and dark glasses. Flat shoes for women and sandals for men were the popular footwear. Beatnik girls were recognizable by their all-black outfits and lavish use of elaborate eye makeup. Black skirts, black leotard tops, and black tights were the beat girl's fashion choice, although wearing the clothes was as close as some would get to the beatnik way of life.

▲Brigitte Bardot: with her smoldering teenage sexuality she was, for Americans in particular, the romance of the Paris Left Bank personified.

Playing It Cool

The beatnik message was, "Be cool." This meant a completely new approach to fashion, and the "right" thing to wear definitely wasn't something from an expensive fashion house. "Being cool" meant being in the know—a very attractive idea for those with limited money to spend. The beatniks' biggest impact on fashion was in this new way of thinking about clothes. As the sixties unfolded, some beatnik attitudes worked their way into the heart of the fashion industry through the boutique and flower power or psychedelic revolutions. These later and much more startling styles of dress were to make the once outrageous beatniks seem almost respectable.

▶A meeting of giants: Bob Dylan with beat poets Michael McLure and Allen Ginsberg.

►A slightly more refined beatnik look for the uptown girl, with tapered pants and oversized shirt.

The Beatles: Pop Goes Fashion

The Mersey Sound

Like all port cities, the Beatles' home town of Liverpool, at the mouth of the Mersey River, had its fair share of visitors, including American seamen, who brought the latest soul and R & B records from the United States. These influences combined with the home-grown "Mersey" sound to produce a music sensation that swept the world in 1963 and lasted for the rest of the decade. At one point, the Beatles held the top four positions in the U.S. singles charts. This was the beginning of the "British Invasion," as groups like the Rolling Stones, the Kinks, Manfred Mann, Herman's Hermits, and The Who quickly followed the Beatles' breakthrough. Successful though these bands were, they couldn't match the popularity of the Beatles, whose concerts could barely be heard above the screams and cries of hysterical girls.

▼The Beatles in their Pierre Cardin suits. This was the look that inspired a revolution—a single-breasted collarless jacket with flapless pockets and pants cut lean, short, and without cuffs. Zip ankle boots and—for 1963—dangerously long hair complete the effect.

▲The effect of this mid-sixties Op Art outfit, with its huge hat and hood, must have been dazzling. Black and white were the simplest and most popular combination of the decade.

Pop Goes Fashion: Fashion Goes Pop

The Beatles took care to keep themselves in the forefront of men's fashion. As with their music, they knew how to move on, changing their style and appeal with each successive record release. Initially, they dressed like typical young men of the sixties, in narrow black trousers and narrow-lapel jackets, and they had cropped hair. But by the time of their breakthrough in 1963, they had adopted the distinctive collarless Cardin suits and collar-length hair that served to make them so instantly recognizable. As the sixties progressed, the Beatles moved on to the psychedelic outfits seen on the jacket of the *Sgt. Pepper* album (1967), ending the decade in the casual hippie look seen on the jacket of *Abbey Road* (1969).

The Beatles also began to attract attention from "serious" music critics. Other musicians who received similar attention included Bob Dylan, Joan Baez and the Rolling Stones. The narrowing of the gap between classical ("serious")

▬ Emanuel Ungaro, a relative newcomer to Paris fashion, proved himself the master of bright, conflicting colors, as this day dress and jacket in striped wool gabardine show.

▲ One of Helmut Newton's Pop Art/Op Art fashion shots for *Queen* magazine, Spring 1966. A new generation of fashion photographers was reshaping the ways in which fashion was presented to the public.

▲ A group put together especially for their own TV series, The Monkees were the American answer to the Beatles. Here they are shown wearing their "uniform" of double-breasted, wine-red shirts, gray slacks, and wide black leather belts.

music and pop was mirrored by some of the changes hitting the world of fashion. As artists like Peter Blake, Richard Hamilton, and Andy Warhol were designing record jackets, Paris designers began to concentrate on their less costly ready-to-wear collections. Images from modern art began to appear on everything from dresses to grocery packaging. Fashion was part of an exciting revolution embracing all the arts.

Pop, Op and Beyond

Op Art and Pop Art were quite different, although equally popular. The Pop Art movement had begun in the fifties, spearheaded by artists like Robert Rauschenberg, Andy Warhol, and Peter Blake. The key was the use of mass-produced, commercial images—from cartoon strips or Warhol's famous soup can—often repeated or enlarged to focus attention on their "deeper" meaning. Pop Art became part and parcel of fashion, its influence continuing on everything from T-shirts to Fiorucci dresses.

Op Art was a separate movement. Painters like Victor Vasarely and Bridget Riley set out to explore and exploit the dramatic, trick-optic effects of line and

◄This 1965 suit by Paris designer Courrèges is heavily influenced by Op Art in its dramatic use of checks. The trademark white boots not only complete the look but easily identify the designer.

▲ This 1966 Young Jaeger outfit of black-and-white mini dress, clear PVC coat, and boots typifies the mid to late 1960s, combining the influence of Op and Pop art with a hint of space age travel. The visored helmet was a little extreme for daily wear, however, even in the sixties.

contrasting areas of color. Designers like Courrèges and Ungaro produced garments heavily influenced by Op Art, while chain stores cashed in on the bold "black-and-white" theme with boots, coats and hats, usually made in vinyl or other artificial fabrics. Bridget Riley's Op Art paintings were used as a basis for a series of textile designs by Julian Tomchin.

The public, however, cheerfully mixed up Op and Pop—to the considerable annoyance of those who had started the movements. Both became just one more set of ideas to be used in the "anything goes" atmosphere of the mid-sixties.

Motown, Mods and Minis

Motown Calling

The early sixties saw the Western world enjoying the benefits of the postwar industrial boom. Teenagers had few problems finding well-paid work. The teenage revolution had been a subject of conversation in the fifties, but now it gathered pace. Young people had become big spenders and were a force to be reckoned with in the fashion business.

In Detroit, Smokey Robinson was spearheading the Motown record company and the new Detroit soul sound. Motown artists were slicker, both in music and in fashion, than the rhythm-and-blues background from which they had emerged. Smokey Robinson and the Miracles, Marvin Gaye, the Supremes, Martha and the Vandellas—all the top Motown acts had an individual style to match their fresh musical approach. Motown became known as "the home of the hits." It stood for a new, sophisticated black style that turned its back on the more rough-and-ready image of the city blues performers like Howling Wolf or Muddy Waters.

▼ Smokey Robinson and the Miracles in 1964, looking elegant in ruffled shirts and pearls. Motown management decreed that all their performers had to be immaculately dressed, whether in performance or off stage.

▲In 1966, Carnaby Street was at the heart of swinging London, and Lord John's was one of its hippest stores.

▲The military look was everywhere: a whole generation of young men who had never been threatened by the draft were suddenly buying up second-hand uniforms.

The March of the Mods

The Motown sound caught on fast in Britain, where the Beatles were its most famous fans, and a new group of teenagers emerged in Britain with a style all their own. The mods took their inspiration from the beatniks and also studied American college fashion for fresh ideas. The results were turtlenecks and brightly colored shirts and ties or, for a more relaxed look, boxy blazers and narrow pants. Mods also favored mohair suits (as worn by the Motown artists) and liked to cover these with a green parka or anorak when out on their Vespa or Lambretta motor scooters, on which they rode around in packs. The Beatles looked a little like mods but always denied any connection with the movement. They wanted to appeal to everyone.

By the mid-sixties, youth culture was enjoying a heyday. Fashion was being made by the young for the young. Small high-fashion shops known as boutiques popped up all over North America and Europe, constantly filled with fresh ideas and new styles. The sales assistants were often teenagers as well, happy to help their contemporaries put together a new look.

Mary Quant understood these trends. She and her husband, Alexander Plunkett-Greene, had been building their design-and-boutique empire since the late fifties, despite having no formal training in business. Quant thrived in the "do-it-yourself" atmosphere of the time. Her clothes were highly original but inexpensive. Although her fabrics weren't always the most practical and the stitching was not the best, young girls could afford to buy one of her outfits almost every week, and the next week they could move on to something new.

In the United States, Betsey Johnson's designs were making a similar impact. Wilder than Quant in some ways, her mid-sixties innovations included clinging T-shirt dresses, silvery motorcycle suits, and a "noise" dress made of jersey with loose grommets attached to the hem for built-in sound effects.

The Mini Makes It Big

Mary Quant played a key role in launching the miniskirt. As a fashion, the mini was worn most effectively by the very young. Teamed up with geometric black-and-white Op Art patterns, the mini became an essential part of the developing mod girl image and quickly spread around the world. While some were shocked by skirts cut eight or nine inches above the knee, others saw the mini as a sign of greater freedom and relaxation in dress.

Models like Twiggy, Jean Shrimpton, and Penelope Tree became

▲Three outfits from 1967 that manage to combine the rebellious schoolgirl look with the essential boyishness of the decade.

◄ The image of the sixties: Twiggy's boyish looks and stick-thin figure made her the number-one model for the miniskirt.

▲Jean Shrimpton, the other face of the sixties, graduated from the famous Lucy Clayton modeling school in 1960, aged just seventeen. She was nicknamed "The Shrimp."

personifications of the new look. Wafer thin, with hair hanging loose or cropped short in the newest Vidal Sassoon cut and youthful, even boyish features, they were very different from most older models, but they fit in perfectly with the new mood. Mary Quant used "Twiggy" mannequins in her chain of boutiques. Young girls tried to copy the "Twiggy look," with huge, heavily made-up eyes, or the "Shrimp look," copying Jean Shrimpton's bangs. Everywhere, old ideas about fashion were being turned upside down. Youth seemed to be taking over completely.

The Space Age

Space Race

Space and space travel had an enormous impact on people's thinking throughout the sixties. Unmanned space missions to Venus and Mars were expanding our knowledge of the solar system, and the USSR and USA were engaged in a race to land the first man on the moon—a race to which the American Apollo 11 mission put a conclusive end on July 20, 1969. In the meantime, space travel had become a major source of inspiration for both the fashion and entertainment industries.

Space Style

Barbarella (1967), starring Jane Fonda, was perhaps the most fashion conscious of space fantasies. Based on a futuristic comic strip, the movie featured bizarre and minimalist outfits in plastic and vinyl, particularly for the women—see-through garments, high boots, and catsuits, with or without leggings. A watered-down form of this look remained high fashion for several years after the movie's release.

TV's *Star Trek* and Stanley Kubrick's film *2001* took a more sober view of the future, a mood reflected by the wardrobe department. The outfits worn by the crews of both the starship *Enterprise* and *2001*'s *Discovery* were actually based on sketches and ideas supplied by NASA scientists, but this didn't stop fans from writing in to ask where they could buy copies of the outfits for themselves.

Space-Age Heroes

Space-age fever caught on at ground level too, with heroes like Batman and James Bond fitting the high-tech mood well. Batman and Robin drove their futuristic Batmobile and dressed in fashionable bodysuits, while arch-villain Catwoman (Eartha Kitt) sported a catsuit—which was only natural. Items like Batman's

◄ Rudi Gernreich's collection of see-through blouses from 1965 onwards was considered very daring. More modest variations simply had see-through, chiffon sleeves.

▲Pierre Cardin dresses from 1967, with typically eccentric headgear loosely based on space helmets.

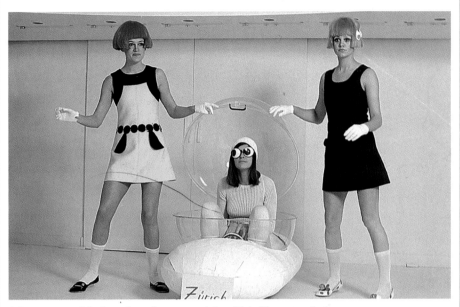

▲Space-age minis from Courrèges, complete with bobby sox and wigs.

SEAN CONNERY IS JAMES BOND

IAN FLEMING'S "YOU ONLY LIVE TWICE"

...and "TWICE" is the only way to live!

▲The unruffled and ultra-charismatic James Bond: proof that "cool" was not the monopoly of the twenty-somethings.

cape and utility belt also seemed more fashion accessories than serious crime-fighting equipment.

Classic James Bond films of the sixties included *Dr. No*, *Goldfinger*, and *You Only Live Twice*, all starring Sean Connery and all placing a strong emphasis on gadgetry, style and humor. *Goldfinger*, for example, opens with two minutes of organized mayhem, from which James Bond emerges unscathed, with a clean tuxedo beneath his rubber wet suit. Bond's stylish adoption of traditional men's garments—dinner jacket, tuxedo, bow tie—created an image for the slightly older man that was both modern and dashing, yet suitable for formal occasions.

Space-Age Haute Couture

However, it was in Europe rather than the USA that the space race made the biggest high-fashion impact. Paco Rabanne, a Spanish-trained architect turned fashion designer, created startling new styles that were widely seen as being "space age" in their approach. Instead of using traditional fabrics, Rabanne used disks cut from metal or plastic, linked by wire. Metallic or neon colors were another key element in his collections.

French designer Pierre Cardin was one of several others to go the space-age route in 1967. Cardin's new styles were much more comfortable and wearable than Rabanne's, even if his catsuits worn with helmets and visors did look like something straight out of the twenty-first century.

Other designers picked up on the "transparent" aspect of the space-age look, made possible by new synthetic fabrics. Rudi Gernreich, originally known as a swimwear designer, produced collections of see-through blouses and dresses in 1968, while in the same year, Courrèges showed plastic dresses with punched holes and Yves Saint Laurent a see-through blouse under a maxi-length coat. The fashion space race was pushing back the boundaries of what was considered acceptable to wear on the street.

▲ *Barbarella*, starring Jane Fonda (1967), was a hit on a galactic scale. Her spacesuit is considerably more comfortable and more appealing than astronaut Buzz Aldrin's, and unlike Aldrin, she's carrying a weapon. Note the Buddhist "yin-yang" symbol on her belt.

▶ Space-age suits for him and her in
Cardin's 1968 autumn/winter show. Gilles's
black leather coverall with zips and silver
strips closely resembles motorcycling gear,
while Therese wears a black felt tunic over
a white turtleneck pullover, with long boots
and a black leather helmet.

▼ *X-Men*, one of Marvel Comics' most
popular titles, was proof that superheroes
had been wearing space-age bodysuits since
Superman burst on the scene in 1938.

The Ethnic Look

Go East

By the later years of the sixties, many young people in the West had begun to take a serious interest in what was happening in the developing world. China had been going through its Cultural Revolution, and many French and British colonies had gained their independence. The "winds of change" were blowing everywhere. The Vietnam War received worldwide media coverage, and it was seen by many young people as senseless killing. There were mass demonstrations against the American government, both within the United States and elsewhere.

The culture of the East impressed the young to the extent that many began to adopt its religions, particularly Buddhism and the beliefs of the Hare Krishna sect—anti-materialist philosophies personified by monks draped in linen. As travel became cheaper, many young people took time out of study for the first time to discover India, Afghanistan, or Indonesia first hand, embarking on the "hippie trail" to the East.

New and Old Roots

Young African Americans were caught up in this mood and began to develop a stronger identity for themselves, with the help of black leaders Dr. Martin Luther King, Jr., Malcolm X, and Huey P. Newton. The political leadership of these men encouraged African Americans to take more pride in their African heritage and to seek to attain a better social standing in a predominantly white society.

▼The black berets, shades, and leather jackets of the Black Panthers, here seen protesting against the murder trial of their leader Huey Newton, were much imitated by young African Americans.

▲Cardin chose the Far East as his inspiration for this sequined ankle-length silk dress.

▶The ethnic origins of this bead dress are finely complemented by the model's "cornrowed" hair, tightly braided into long strips.

Fashionable clothing reflected all these movements, and many designs had a heavy ethnic influence. Afghans led to caftans. African Americans favored the unisex "dashiki," based on the loose-fitting, vividly colored and printed African tunic. Transparent silks in bold prints were draped freely around the body, flaunting their contrast to traditional Western cut and shape.

Beaded accessories were on sale in even the most elegant stores. Fringe and tassel dresses, worn with a headband and reminiscent of native American dress, were shown at fashion shows and sold in exclusive stores. Youngsters carried brightly colored woven bags imported from Morocco and Turkey and wore flat leather sandals, also imported. Ethnic fashion was fanciful and unselfconscious: it left plenty of room for individual interpretation and did not bother too much about which part of the world each piece of exotica might have come from.

Fashion for Pharaohs

Courrèges devised an ethnic look that took its ideas from the ancient Egyptians. Outfits made from heavily sequined bands held together by transparent silk suggested the wrappings of mummified pharaohs, and to finish off the look, Courrèges gave his models squared-off bobbed wigs in metallic colors.

The phrase "black is beautiful" was first coined in 1968, when young African Americans were developing their own style of revolutionary fashion. They stopped using chemicals to straighten their natural curls, resulting in the "afro" hairstyle—traditional African hair grown to its maximum length and shaped

▼New Mexico hippies in 1968, wrapped in blankets or ponchos that suggest an origin south of the border.

◄ Yves Saint Laurent was certainly under the influence of Africa when he designed this collection, as the jewelry and the hairstyles confirm.

▼ The ever-changing face of Diana Ross: in 1968, she was sporting a fashionable afro.

evenly. This was to catch on far and wide, with white contemporaries frizzing their locks in imitation. Even young Japanese raced to hairdressers to acquire an afro. Some even wore afro wigs in bright colors to join in with this new, exotic image. The leaders of the trend had been African American pop and soul stars, with some—like Sylvester Stewart, "Sly" of Sly and the Family Stone—sporting the most spectacular hairstyles of all.

Olympic Protest

Che Guevara, the Argentine-born Cuban revolutionary hero, became a model for thousands of radical students, while many young African-Americans were influenced by the military-style clothing and trademark black berets of the Black Panthers. When winning athletes stood on the podium at the 1968 Mexico Olympics and gave the Panthers' clenched fist salute instead of saluting the Stars and Stripes, the popularity of the movement was given a further boost.

◄ The photograph of Che Guevara by Alberto Korda became the most famous image in the world. An international symbol of the struggle for freedom, it appeared on posters and on T-shirts worn by students all over the world.

▲Athletes give the Black Power salute in a demonstration at the 1968 Olympic Games.

Psychedelic Explosion

The "Underground"

Music was the main force behind the psychedelic explosion of the late sixties, a burst of activity in music, fashion, art—and other events and "happenings"—never seen before.

Many of the ideas underlying this movement had first surfaced in San Francisco, but the mood of the times was international, and ideas seemed to sweep along an invisible grapevine—the "underground." Underground magazines, groups and festivals sprang up all over America and Europe during 1966 and 1967.

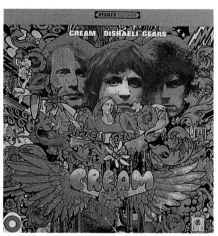

▲Cream's *Disraeli Gears* from 1968 was the ultimate in psychedelia.

◄ Striped pants, waistcoat, T-shirt, "granny" glasses, love-beads, droopy mustache, and long hair—almost a uniform for musicians and their hangers-on in the late sixties.

►Fabric designed by Emilio Pucci in the late sixties. Sharp, brilliantly glowing "acid" colors became a trademark of Italy's noted designer.

▼Jimi Hendrix, psychedelic standard-bearer and probably the best electric guitarist in the world, died at the height of his fame in 1970.

A number of young talents died tragically at the pinnacle of their careers, including Janis Joplin, Otis Redding, Jimi Hendrix, and Brian Jones. For the first time, marijuana and hallucinogens like LSD, previously limited to a small circle of artists and musicians, were being more widely used. It was a time of boundless experimentation in the arts, lifestyle, and fashion—epitomized by Bob Dylan's album *Blonde on Blonde.*

▲ *Oz* was one of the most famous of the underground magazines of the late sixties, featuring psychedelic graphics coupled with the early writings of Germaine Greer, Clive James, and others.

◄ Janis Joplin, one of the troubled casualties of 1960s free-wheeling permissiveness, at the Woodstock festival in 1969.

Bold as Love

Psychedelic music took its inspiration from everywhere—the blues, jazz, rock, electronic music, Indian music and even the classical tradition. One of the era's iconic figures was guitarist and singer Jimi Hendrix.

Hendrix had begun his career as a backup musician for rhythm and blues singers like Little Richard. He found stardom after he moved to London in 1966, capturing the hearts and minds of London's underground club circuit. He later returned to the United States, causing a sensation at the Monterey Pop Festival with his onstage guitar-burning routine.

▲The Beatles meet their cardboard alter egos in a publicity shot for the movie *Yellow Submarine* (1968), which cleverly packaged the psychedelic mood for the mass market. Although they began their flower power phase in these designer outfits, by the following year the Beatles were dressing more like the average hippie next door.

▼Four bright young things of the late sixties on a country weekend, all printed velvet, embroidery, and floppy scarves.

Also a trendsetter in his dress, Hendrix's colorful and exotic shirts and vests, boots, wide-brimmed hats and elaborate jewelry were frequently photographed by fashion magazines. But many saw Hendrix as a "wild man" and a dangerous Pied Piper, whose appearance alone was enough to start teenagers on a rampage of drugs, long hair, and loud music. Hendrix was to die under mysterious circumstances in 1970.

Janis Joplin, with her own brand of raw energy and a strong, gutsy voice influenced by early blues singers, was the female personification of the psychedelic period. Just as outrageous as Jimi Hendrix in her lifestyle, she seemed on the verge of international stardom at the time of her death in 1970.

Graphic artists like Peter Max also acquired a taste for psychedelia. There was a broad turning away from self-conscious minimalism and Op Art toward fantasies that used vivid "acid" colors and cartoon imagery. Posters and, above all, album covers reflected this trend.

Sgt. Pepper

Male dress was becoming increasingly fancy and feminine, with flouncy shirts in fluorescent colors, brightly printed neck scarves, and beaded belts. The Beatles' costumes on the *Sgt. Pepper* album jacket (1967) are a classic example of psychedelic dress for men—brightly colored old-style military uniforms, in which the band posed like flower-power Napoleons. In making even these kinds of clothes into a psychedelic statement, the Beatles undercut a stronghold of masculine conformity. Appearing at the height of the Vietnam War, the significance of these freaked-out uniforms would not have been lost on fans.

Fashion designers responded to the psychedelic mood by strengthening their colors. Bright and bold purple and orange flower prints on velvet fabrics were made into tight-fitting trousers for men. The trend was completely international. Italian designer Emilio Pucci gave his clothes both a richness of color and brilliant patterns, making use of newly devised stretch fabrics in his tight-fitting dresses and trousers.

Fiorucci developed an equally youthful approach to fashion, using pop styles to create his own particular brand of chic. Bright colors and animal prints on dresses and skirts remained his hallmark even in the eighties. Psychedelia lives on.

Flower Power Goes High Fashion

▲ A happy hippie wedding, 1968.

▼ Members of Hog Farm Commune, El Rito, New Mexico taking part in the Fourth of July Parade in 1969.

The Hippie Dream

The original hippies living in San Francisco in the mid-sixties could not have imagined that by the end of the decade, their crazy style of dressing would have become high fashion. Theirs was an "anti-style," which rejected the whole work ethic of Western society along with its conformist clothing. Hippies had shocked and intrigued with their communal lifestyles, belief in free love, and experiments with drugs. Tourists flocked to San Francisco's Haight-Ashbury neighborhood to see these strange beings in sandals and caftans, handing out flowers as symbols of peace and love. Others talked of an alternative society and of establishing self-supporting rural communities of like-minded people.

In complete contrast to the clean, geometric lines of the "space-age" look, hippies decorated everything, even painting their bodies. The psychedelic, the ethnic, and a romanticized view of the past all jostled together. The hippie

woman would not wear a teasing miniskirt, but a floor-length skirt accessorized with love beads and bells. The hippie man, with flowing robe and long, loose hair, presented much the same outline, challenging society's ideas about masculinity. "You can't tell the boys from the girls!" was the outraged response.

But it wasn't necessary to be a full-time hippie. By 1967—the "Summer of Love"—the fashionable youth of America and Europe had taken up the hippie look, although not always the hippie way of life. In an era of increasing affluence, they could afford to show contempt for money while continuing to work. *Hair*, the "tribal love-rock musical," opened on Broadway in April 1968 and then went on to London, proving a smash hit everywhere.

Hair and Hemlines

Everyone started to grow their hair long. By 1969, even the well-groomed Twiggy wanted hers to her waist. Long hair on boys, however, was often discouraged or banned in schools. The Beatles continued to grow their hair still longer, and they adopted not only hippie fashions but much of the hippie philosophy. In January 1968, they set up Apple Corps Ltd., an attempt to organize business on terms of complete trust. The Apple boutique in London opened to great fanfare and the fashions were featured in *Vogue*, but it closed before the end of the year with huge losses.

The long maxi-skirt, a hippie spin-off, aroused much the same anger as the mini. Many girls cashed in on this by flaunting both fashions, wearing the shortest of skirts under the longest of coats.

The Designer Hippie

Paris designers flung themselves into the new mood with enthusiasm. The hippies' cheap, flamboyant clothes were transformed into expensive designer wear embraced by the establishment. The ready-to-wear collections of January 1967 were full of oriental touches—striped djellabas, harem dresses, tent dresses, rajah coats, and Nehru jackets, all in fine wools and exotic silks.

Jewelry collections for men were launched for wear over loose, billowing shirts and wide-bottomed velvet trousers. The look was soft and feminine. For women, Yves Saint Laurent produced long highwayman coats. Everyone could dress up in the style of another country, another age, another sex. Anti-fashion had become the biggest fashion of all.

By 1969, hard-and-fast rules no longer seemed to exist. Some designers, notably Courrèges, persevered with the short, sharp mini, and the "space-age" look was given a new lease on life when Apollo 11 landed men on the moon. But most people began to subscribe to the hippie ideal of "doing your own thing." "The length of your skirt is how you feel this moment," reported *Vogue*. The designers agreed, and the final collections of the sixties embraced the micro-skirt and the maxi, along with the compromise midi. Anti-fashion had triumphed in a roundabout way, and nothing would ever be quite the same again.

▲ Those who couldn't afford a Bentley like John Lennon's just repainted their VW Beetle.

▶ To enjoy the best of both worlds, a girl went for the shortest of minis under one of the new-length maxi-coats.

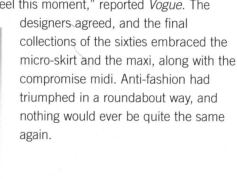

◀ The inspiration for this caftan, designed by Vancetti for spring 1969, may have been Turkey, but the hairstyle is undeniably African.

Andy Warhol

▲New York's Velvet Underground gained pop culture's ultimate seal of approval with this album cover by artist and style guru Andy Warhol.

Chronology

1960 **News**
American U2 spy plane shot down over USSR.
John F. Kennedy elected US President.
Rome Olympics held.

1961 Berlin Wall goes up.
Stalin's body removed from Red Square in Moscow.
Yuri Gagarin first man in space.

1962 Arrest of ANC leader Nelson Mandela in South Africa.
John Glenn achieves first US orbital space flight.
Cuba missile crisis.

1963 Profumo scandal in Britain.
Alec Douglas Home becomes British Prime Minister.
President Kennedy assassinated: Lyndon Johnson becomes US President.

1964 Trial of Nelson Mandela.
Labour Party wins elections in Britain: Harold Wilson becomes Prime Minister.

1965 Watts riots in Los Angeles.
Lyndon Johnson takes Kennedy's Civil Rights Bill through Congress.

1966 France leaves NATO.
Cultural Revolution officially begins in China.

1967 Six Day War in the Middle East.

1968 Tet Offensive in Vietnam: US involvement reaches its peak.
Assassination of Robert Kennedy and Martin Luther King Jr.

1969 Border clashes between USSR and China.
The "Troubles" begin in Northern Ireland.
US Apollo 11 astronauts land on moon.

Events

Fellini's *La Dolce Vita* and Hitchcock's *Psycho* among the new movies released.
Marc Bolan becomes artistic director for Dior.

Plans made to save Egypt's Abu Simbel temples, threatened by rising waters from the Aswan dam.

"Love Me Do," the first Beatles single.
Dr No, the first James Bond movie, released

Beatlemania erupts as the group tops charts around the world.
Peak of folk music scene in US: Bob Dylan and Joan Baez are leading exponents.

Beatles achieve top four positions in US singles charts.
"British Invasion" of brands follows in the Beatles' wake.

Antonioni's *The Red Desert* and Richard Lester's *The Knack* are two of the year's most talked-about movies.
Bob Dylan "goes electric," infuriating many folk music fans.

Psychedelic movement in music and fashion gathers pace.

Beatles release *Sgt. Pepper*, a psychedelic record inside a psychedelic pop art cover.
Sci fi movie *Barbarella* and gangster movie *Bonnie and Clyde* are both hugely successful.

Beatles' movie *Yellow Submarine* opens; Beatles' Apple boutique opens and closes.
Black Power demonstrations by medal-winning US athletes at the Mexico Olympics.
2001: A Space Odyssey released.

Peace and love triumphant at Woodstock festival.

Fashion

Courrèges opens his own house.
Emmanuelle Khanh achieves prominence in France, with designs featured in *Elle* magazine.

Saint Laurent opens his own business.
Dorothée Bis chain opens.

Cardin designs "Beatle suits."
Mary Quant starts Ginger Group label.
Geoffrey Beene forms his own company.

Rudi Gernreich Inc. formed.
Cardin's "Space Age" collection.

Mini-skirts climb far above the knee.
Plastic dress from Paco Rabanne.
Betsey Johnson makes impact as designer while working as editor for *Madamoiselle* magazine.

Saint Laurent opens Rive Gauche ready-to-wear chain. His couture collection features a "smoking" jacket for women.
Paco Rabanne forms his own label.
Twiggy emerges as the decade's most famous model.

Fiorucci begins expanding his family business.
Psychedelic and ethnic fashions begin to appear in the designer collections.

Balenciaga retires.
Saint Laurent shows see-through blouse and safari jacket.

Afro hairstyles begin to catch on universally.
Maxi and midi lengths begin to gain ground.
Saint Laurent introduces pantsuits.

Glossary

Afro Naturally grown, long, bushy hairstyle widely adopted by African-Americans in the 1960s. Artificially created, it also became popular among whites during the late sixties and early seventies.

Apple Corps Ltd. Organization set up by the Beatles in 1968 to control their own record label as well as other business and artistic ventures, including two Apple boutiques in London. Apple Corps and the boutiques folded after less than a year, though the record label survived.

Barbarella Film directed by Roger Vadim. Released in 1967, it features Jane Fonda as an interplanetary adventurer, and features fantastic and innovative space-age costumes designed by Jaques Fonteray.

Bates, John (b. 1935) British designer. Worked as a fashion illustrator in the fifties before forming the Varnon company in 1964, producing an exciting range of youthful designs, including pantsuits, catsuits and string-vest dresses. Bates also designed costumes for the Emma Peel character in TV series *The Avengers*.

Beene, Geoffrey (1927-2004) American designer. Worked in New York. In 1963 set up his own company, gaining a reputation for his simple, youthful shifts and T-shirt dresses. Other influential work in the late sixties included designs with sequined fabrics, chiffon, jersey and taffeta.

Cardin, Pierre (b. 1922) French designer. Worked with Paquin, Schiaparelli and Dior before producing his first collection in 1957. His career blossomed in the sixties, with cut-out dresses, space-age catsuits, tight leather pants, bodystockings and other concepts that became inseparable from "space-age" sixties fashion.

Cashin, Bonnie (1915-2000) US designer, born in Oakland, California. Worked in costume design for Hollywood before opening her own fashion business in New York in 1949. A great mixer of fabrics, especially leather, canvas and suede, and a clever adapter of ethnic influences, Cashin's work was an important influence on the direction of sixties fashion, and on the fashions of later years.

Chanel, Gabrielle "Coco" (1883-1971) French designer. Designed under her own label from 1914. Extremely influential and innovative in the twenties, thirties and later through her introduction of the "Chanel suit." By the sixties, the Chanel suit had re-emerged to gain the classic status it still enjoys today.

Clark, Ossie (1942-1996) British designer. Working for the Quorum boutique from the early sixties, Clark was an influential figure on the Kings Road fashion scene throughout the decade, producing gypsy dresses, motorcycle jackets and innovative work in leather and snakeskin.

Courrèges, André (b. 1923) French designer. Worked for Balenciaga before opening his own house in 1961. A leading figure in the introduction of the mini-skirt and pants suit, Courrèges also became known as a space-age designer for his catsuits, see-through dresses and futuristic goggles and boots. A key figure in sixties fashion.

Dior, Christian (1905-1957) French designer. Revolutionized postwar fashion with his New Look of 1947. After Dior's death, the House of Dior was led by French designer Marc Bohan (b.1926), who successfully carried Dior's reputation for elegance into the decade of pop fashions.

Djellabah Moroccan hooded cloak with long, wide sleeves, worn open at the neck and reaching to the knee.

Dorothée Bis Chain of stores opened by Elie and Jaqueline Jacobson in Paris and later in the USA. From 1962 the chain specialized in adult versions of young girls' clothes, including knee socks, peaked caps and ribbed knitwear.

Fiorucci, Elio (b. 1935) Italian designer and entrepreneur, born in Milan. Fiorucci inherited a shoe store from his father, and soon expanded the shop's stock to include mini-skirts. Opened a larger store in 1967 and from this base built up his world-famous chain of boutiques for the young consumer.

Fogarty, Anne (1919-1981) American designer. Worked for many clients, including Saks Fifth Avenue, for whom she designed from 1957. A significant influence in the fifties, Fogarty responded creatively to the challenge of the sixties with culottes, mini-skirts and other simple, wearable designs.

Gernreich, Rudi (1922-1985) Austrian-born designer. Worked in the USA from 1938, designing under his own name from 1951. In 1964 formed Rudi Gernreich Inc. Best remembered today for swimwear and underwear, including bodystockings and radically engineered bras for low-neck and plunge-back evening wear, but also an influential designer of sportswear, separates and shirtwaists.

Givenchy, Hubert (b. 1927) French designer. Worked for Schiaparelli before opening his own business in 1952. An important influence on the elegant cocktail and evening dress look of the late fifties and early sixties, Givenchy's designs were a favorite with (amongst others) first lady Jackie Kennedy.

Johnson, Betsey (b. 1942) American designer, born in Hartford, Connecticut. In 1964, became an editor at *Mademoiselle* magazine, while designing clothes in her spare time, and by 1965 was widely hailed as a radical and exciting new designer. Continued to innovate through the sixties, with pantsuits, mini-skirts, T-shirt dresses, and many other novelties. Opened her own New York boutique called "Betsey, Bunky and Mini" in 1969, and turned to designing disco and sportswear.

Khanh, Emmanuelle (b. 1937) French designer. Worked for Dorothée Bis and Cacharel in the sixties, establishing her own label in 1970. Sixties designs included long, droopy collars on jackets, dresses and blouses, frilly mini-skirts, and lined outfits with lace trimming. Associated with the French "Ye Ye" fashions of the sixties, which took their nickname from the Beatles' song "She Loves You, Yeah Yeah Yeah."

Nehru Jacket Straight, slim, hip-length jacket, buttoned in front to a straight, standing collar. Based on the design of a jacket popularized by Jawaharlal Nehru, Indian prime minister 1947-1964.

Op Art Art movement prominent in the 1960s, and extremely influential on fashion and textile design. Op Art exploits the dramatic "trick optic" effects of contrasting areas of color and black-and-white.

Parka Hooded garment similar to an anorak, but usually longer and more loosely-cut. Popular outerwear for mods.

Pop Art Art movement having its origins in the fifties, but very widely influential on fashion and much else in the sixties. Pop Art makes use of ready-made images from consumer society, concentrating the viewer's attention by enlarging them or offering them in a startling new context.

Pucci, Emilio (b. 1914) Italian designer. A doctor of political science and member of the Italian Olympic skiing team, Pucci entered the fashion world by designing sportswear. His boldly patterned fabrics for skirts, dresses and pantsuits brilliantly captured the psychedelic mood of the late sixties.

Quant, Mary (b. 1934) British designer. Opened her first shop in 1955, and founded the Ginger Group label in 1963. Quant's bright, simple and well-coordinated designs were perfectly in tune with the mood of the 1960s. Innovations included the mini-skirt, colored tights, skinny-rib sweaters and a range of wet-look vinyl fashions.

Rabanne, Paco (b. 1934) Spanish designer. Studied architecture in Paris, 1952-1964, and architectural background led to dresses made from plastic, metal discs and chains instead of conventional fabrics. Opened his own house in 1966, and continued to be a key influence on the space age styles of the decade.

Ready-to-Wear Clothes carrying a designer label that can be bought ready-made from the hanger.

Saint Laurent, Yves (b. 1936) French designer. Worked successfully for Christian Dior before opening his own house in 1962. His inventive genius was ideally matched to the mood of the sixties, producing a seemingly endless parade of startling but much-imitated designs: pea jackets, smocks in jersey and silk, knickerbockers, see-through blouses, pantsuits, and safari suits. Opened his own ready-to-wear chain, Rive Gauche, in 1966. Remains a key figure in the development of modern fashion.

Further Reading

A great deal has been written and published about the 1960s, and this reading list is only a very small selection. Magazines and movies of the period are another excellent source of information.

Adult General Reference Sources

Calasibetta, Charlotte. *Essential Terms of Fashion: A Collection of Definitions* (Fairchild, 1985)

Calasibetta, Charlotte. *Fairchild's Dictionary of Fashion* (Fairchild, 2nd ed, 1988)

Cumming, Valerie. *Understanding Fashion History* (Chrysalis, 2004)

Ewing, Elizabeth. *History of Twentieth Century Fashion,* revised by Alice Mackrell (Batsford, 4th ed, 2001)

Gold, Annalee. *90 Years of Fashion* (Fairchild, 1990)

O'Hara, Georgina. *The Encyclopedia of Fashion* (Harry N. Abrams, 1986)

Olian, JoAnne. *Everyday Fashions of the Sixties* (Dover, 1999)

Peacock, John. *Fashion Sourcebooks: The 1960s* (Thames & Hudson, 1998)

Peacock, John. *Men's Fashion: The Complete Sourcebook* (Emerald, 1997)

Peacock, John. *Fashion Accessories: The Complete 20th Century Sourcebook* (Thames & Hudson, 2000)

Skinner, Tina. *Fashionable Clothing from the Sears Catalogs* (Schiffer, 2004)

Steele, Valerie. *Fifty Years of Fashion: New Look to Now* (Yale, 2000)

Stegemeyer, Anne. *Who's Who in Fashion*, (Fairchild, 4th ed, 2003)

Trahey, Jane (ed.) Harper's Bazaar: *100 Years of the American Female* (Random House, 1967)

Watson, Linda. *Twentieth-century Fashion* (Firefly, 2004)

Young Adult Sources

Powe-Temperley, Kitty. *Twentieth Century Fashion: the 60s* (Heinemann Library, 1999)

Ruby, Jennifer. *The Nineteen Sixties & Nineteen Seventies, Costume in Context* series (David & Charles, 1989)

Wilcox, R. Turner. *Five Centuries of American Costume* (Scribner's, 1963)

Acknowledgments

The Publishers would like to thank the following for permission to reproduce illustrations: B.T. Batsford 11r, 20, 30r, 31, 32t, 35, 39l, 45b, 46, 47l, 49l, 51r, 52, 53t, 54r, 58b; Camera Press 10, 25, 28r, 29l, 38tr, 42b, 49r, 55t, 57, 58tl; David Redfern 27, 54l; Kobal Collection 8r; Museum of Costumes in Bath 39; NASA 11l; Popperfoto 8l, 9, 14l, 16, 23, 36, 42t; Rex Features 12t, 13, 14r, 15, 17, 18, 24b, 30l, 33, 34t, 37, 38br, 39r, 40, 41, 45tr, 53b, 58tr; Topfoto 6, 7, 12b, 19, 21, 22, 24t, 28l, 29r, 32b, 34b, 44, 45tl, 47r, 48, 50, 51l, 55b, 56, 59; Victoria & Albert Museum 38l, 43

Key: b=bottom, t=top, l=left, r=right

Index

Figures in italics refer to illustrations.

Abbey Road 37
Africa 6, 21, 24, 48, 49, 50, 51
afro hairstyle 24, 26, 50, *50,* 51
Ali, Muhammad *22*
Apollo missions *11,* 26, 44, 58
Apple boutique 57. *57*
Apple Corps Ltd. 57
Avengers, The 14

Baez, Joan 20, *22,* 37
Balenciaga, Cristobal 8, 26
Balmain, Pierre 32
Barbarella 44, 46
Bardot, Brigitte 32, *34*
Batman 44
Beach Boys 18, *19*
Beatlemania 12
Beatles, The 6, 36, *36,* 37, 38, 41, 55, *55*
beatniks *8, 9, 32,* 34, *35*
beehives 29, *30*
Beene, Geoffrey 18
Black Power 24, *51*
Blake, Peter 38
Blonde on Blonde 53
Bond, James 30, 44, *45, 46*
Brown, James 26
Buddhism 48
Byrd, Donald *32*

caftans 49, 56, 58
California 9, 18, 22, 24
Cardin, Pierre 6, 26, *36,* 37, *45, 46, 47, 49,* 51
Carnaby Street *41*
Cashin, Bonnie 26
Chanel, Coco 17, 26, 28
China 20, 48
Courrèges, André 26, *39, 45,* 46, 58
Cream *52*

dashikis 49

Day, Doris *29,* 30
Dior, Christian 8, *10,* 17, 28, *31*
Disraeli Gears 52
djellabas 58
Dylan, Bob 6, *6, 7, 34,* 37, 53

Egyptian style 50

Ferlinghetti, Lawrence 9
Fiorucci, Elio 26, 38, 53
Fogarty, Anne 18
Fonda, Jane 44, *46*

Gaye, Marvin 40
Gernreich, Rudi 17, *44,* 46
Ginsberg, Allen 9, 34, *34*
Givenchy, Hubert 8
Greco, Juliette 32, *33*
Guevara, Che *51*

Haight-Ashbury 56
Hair 52, 57
Hamilton, Richard 38
Hare Krishna 48
haute couture 7, *10*
Hayes, Isaac 26
Hendrix, Jimi 6, 26, 28, 53, 54, 55
hippies 26, *50,* 56, *56,* 57, 58
Howling Wolf 40

India 18, 48, 54

Jackson, Michael 6
Jagger, Mick 6, 26
Japan 6, 26, 51
Johnson, Betsey 17, *18,* 26, 41
Jones, Brian 53
Joplin, Janis 6, 26, 53, *54,* 55

Kennedy, Jackie 28, *28*
Kennedy, John F. 11, 18, 20, 21, 28
Kerouac, Jack 9, 34
King, Dr. Martin Luther 18, *21,* 48
Kinks 36
Kitt, Eartha 44

Kubrick, Stanley 11, 44

Lanvin, Jeanne 8
Little Richard 54
Liverpool 6, 36
London 8, 26, 41, 54, 57
LSD 53

Malcom X 48
Manfred Mann 36
Marvel Comics 47
Mashed Potato 30
Martha and the Vandellas 26, 40
Max, Peter 55
maxi-skirts 58
micro-skirts 58
miniskirts 15, 20, 42, *42,* 58, *59*
mods 12, *12,* 18, 40, 41
Monkees, The *38*
Monterey Pop Festival 54
Morocco 49
Motown 6, 40, 41
Muddy Waters 40

Nehru jackets 58
New York 9, 26, 58
Newton, Helmut *38*
Newton, Huey 21, 48
Nixon, Richard 18, 26

On the Road 34
Op Art 26, *37,* 38, *39,* 42, 55
Oz 54

Paris 9, 18, *24,* 26, 28, 32, 33
parkas 12
Plunkett-Greene, Alexander 41
Pop Art *38*
Powe, Hector *30*
Presley, Elvis 31
Pucci, Emilio 26, 53, 55

Quant, Mary 13, 15, *16,* 17, *17,* 41, 42, 43

Rabanne, Paco 46
Rauschenberg, Robert 38
Redding, Otis 53

Riley, Bridget 38
Rive Gauche *15,* 17, *17*
Robinson, Smokey 6, 40
Rolling Stones, The 6, *9,* 26, 36, 37
Ronettes, The *30*
Ross, Diana 6, *50*

Saint Laurent, Yves 6, 8, 15, 17, *17,* 26, 28, 46, *50,* 58
San Francisco 34, 52, 56
Santana 26
Sassoon, Vidal 43
Sgt. Pepper 6, 37, 43, 55
Sly and the Family Stone *24,* 26, 51
Star Trek 44
Superman 47
Supremes, The 6, *7,* 40, *40*
suspense jupe 28, *28*

Truffaut, François 32
Turkey 49, 58
Twiggy *13, 42,* 43, 57
Twist 30
2001 11, 44

"underground", the 52, 54
Ungaro, Emanuel *38*
unisex dressing 24
USA 11, 17, 19, 20, 21, 22, 23, 36, 41, 48, 54
USSR 11, 20, 44

Vadim, Roger 32
Vancetti *25,* 26, *58*
Vasarely, Victor 38
Velvet Underground *58*
Vietnam 20, 21, 22, *23,* 48, 55
Vogue 16, 57, 58

Warhol, Andy 38, *58*
West Side Story 8, 9
Who, The 26
Wonder, Stevie 6
Woodstock 26, *27*

X-Men 47

Yellow Submarine 55